Joe & Sue Monaco
2247 Lewis Road
Poultney Vt 05764
802·236·0231

SENDOUTCARDS

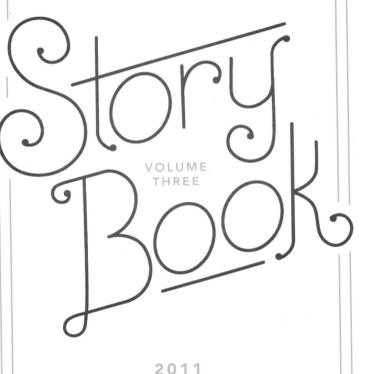

Story

VOLUME
THREE

Book

2011

SendOutCards Story Book, Volume Three ©2011 Send Out Cards, LLC.

Story Collection: Michelle Bateman
Writers: Rebecca Long Pyper, Paul Kempski
Design: Nicholas Wheeler
Production/Printing: Jorge Bernal
Editor: Melody Marler Forshée

Printed in the United States of America.

ISBN: 978-1-936677-09-2

Changing Lives... One Card at a Time

1825 Research Way
Salt Lake City, UT 84119
801-463-3800
www.sendoutcards.com

SendOutCards® is a company built on stories. Almost every day, we hear stories about how someone mended a relationship, solidified a business alliance, overcame adversity, or made a difference in someone's life, through using or sharing the SendOutCards opportunity.

KODY BATEMAN
Founder and CEO,
SendOutCards

A few months ago we asked our SendOut-Cards family to share their heartfelt stories with us. The collection of stories you hold in your hands is a result of that outreach, and is the third in a series of Story Books prepared for our Annual Convention (volumes 1 and 2 were released at earlier conventions).

The strongest businesses are built on heartfelt, unique, sincere stories. As the economy puts stress on everyone, there are more people looking for opportunity and a chance to make a difference, to send out kindness and gratitude right now — more than ever before. Be proud of the opportunity you have to share. We are network marketing at its very best. Thank you for helping us continue to write stories of freedom, success, hope, and love.

Your friend,

CONTENTS

PLAYGROUNDS OF PEACE

· MARK WHITE ·

Mark White was an average guy, married to his high school sweetheart Nancy, with two great kids. The family lived in Missouri and Mark had a job he loved, designing playgrounds for the local school system.

But like so many, Mark was looking for a way to increase his income to provide extra security for his family. That's when he was introduced to SendOutCards. He immediately signed up as a distributor.

He had little time to immediately build his business, as he left for a planned trip to Poland soon after signing up. It was a wonderful vacation, filled with wonder and discovery of a magical new land. Yet the real magic was just beginning.

While exploring the country, Mark came upon a school playground. Naturally, he was interested and stopped to take a closer look. A beautiful young girl was doing her best to enjoy herself, playing on an old, rusted, unsafe swing set. An expert in the field, Mark was horrified. He was touched more deeply when he learned that the school was actually an orphanage.

That's the moment when Mark's life changed forever. He decided to contact all of his playground equipment and construction vendors in the United States, with a plan to return to Poland and build suitable, safe playgrounds. All of Mark's contacts were more than happy to help, and soon he returned to Poland, where he was able to build a magnificent new playground at the orphanage.

The orphanage staff and children were more than grateful at this seemingly impossible gift. Yet it was Mark and his family who received the greatest gift of all, when they adopted Ania, the little girl Mark had seen that first day on the dangerous playground equipment. Ania and her brother David joined their new family in America.

Mark's industry stalled somewhat when the economy did, and he was concerned that contributions to his new organization, Playgrounds of Peace ("POPs") would dry up. He was scheduled to leave soon for Nepal, to build yet another playground.

Undeterred, Mark simply sent "thank you" cards to all of the companies that had helped create the new playgrounds in foreign lands up to that point. The cards included photos of children playing and carried a simple "thank you" message.

Several weeks later Mark received a phone call. The president of a major manufacturer of playground equipment had kept the card on his desk and couldn't get it out of his mind. Mark was happy the man was so touched, but he was totally unprepared for this man said next.

"Mark, every year our company chooses one organization to which we donate $10,000. This year we've chosen Playgrounds of Peace." Mark was thrilled that the Nepal playground could be built and the organization would continue to spread joy to less fortunate children around the world.

Mark attributes much of his success to SendOutCards. That simple gesture of gratitude has paid off many times over, not just for Mark but for the children. "I absolutely know that SendOutCards is the pathway to my dreams," said Mark.

FROM HOMELESS TO HOPE

· TIM & NICOLE MANCUSO ·

Joining the SendOutCards family was a once, twice, third time's the charm for the Mancuso family. In the beginning, Tim showed the SendOutCards opportunity to his wife Nicole. Tim had been laid off three times, but had just landed a great new job, so Nicole was less than enthusiastic about him spending time on working a SendOutCards business.

"I wanted him to focus on the new job while I homeschooled our children," Nicole said. A deeply religious family, the couple prayed about it and felt prompted to go ahead with the business opportunity. So in November 2008 they spent the last of their savings to join SendOutCards.

In one month's time, Tim was laid off. Although the couple had reached the rank of Senior Manager, they lost their home and had to move in with friends. Tim soon found another job, but it took the focus off building their SendOutCards business.

"In November of 2009 I was picking up some Thanksgiving food a friend was kind enough to give us and found myself pleading with God, 'HELP US!' I was met with a strange feeling," Nicole said. "It felt like we had already been given the answer."

Tim was laid off again in January. This time, though, the couple took

the time and energy to refocus on their SendOutCards business, and ended up winning the trip to Cancun in April 2010.

"Every good thing led to another," Nicole said. "A year after we officially became homeless, we found ourselves moving into our own home."

Despite their success in SendOutCards, their friends and family kept encouraging the couple to find a "real job," temporarily once again distracting them from their focus on SendOutCards.

"We won the trip in 2011 to Florida," Nicole said. "It was there that we both felt clear direction to focus on our business first and foremost, and we have been full-time with SendOutCards from that time. We still have a lot to do. But now we have a vision and hope for our future. We look forward to helping others find freedom and share the hope we have found, through God and SendOutCards, for their own futures. We **will** be Eagles in SendOutCards — we will be **free!**"

I ONLY HAVE EYES FOR YOU

· STEPHEN FESWICK ·

When newcomer Stephen Feswick first saw SendOutCards, he was sold. His wife Pam, however, was not.

Stephen's five previous unsuccessful attempts at network marketing left Pam feeling suspicious about him reentering the world of multilevel marketing.

But Stephen had a plan. The first SendOutCards greeting card he sent went straight to Pam, along with the words "I only have eyes for you." Those words weren't just familiar to Pam; they were sentimental.

"This was the first song played for us at our wedding in 1975," Stephen said. "When her card arrived in the mail, she opened it and read the message I had written inside. Through her tears she told me, 'You must do this business!'"

This new career opportunity wasn't Stephen's first experience with greeting cards. A longtime fan of direct sales, Stephen began his career at age 12, selling greeting cards door to door. "Now some 43 years later I find myself once again happily involved in the greeting card industry with SendOutCards," he said.

Even with that enthusiasm, working in general isn't easy for Stephen or Pam. For three years he's been "out of commission," he said, overcoming Stage IV Hodgkin's disease. And now that he's in full remission, Pam has been diagnosed with Leiomyosarcoma, an incurable form of cancer.

"We are, of course, challenged by our circumstances. But as I now return to the workplace I can't imagine a more valuable business opportunity I could offer to the world," he said. "For me, success has already been realized by the lives touched through my heartfelt messages. In a good way, I've made more people cry in the past few months than during my entire life to date. I expect to do more of the same going forward."

HOPE IN STRESSFUL TIMES

· KIM WELCH ·

In 2009 Kim Welch had just started a new and passionate career in life insurance — a career that was demanding 60 hours a week — and found herself earning $10,000 a month but becoming more ill as days clicked by.

The stress brought on a bad flare of ulcerative colitis. Before long, Kim was uninsurable and eventually admitted to the hospital, away from her kids and her husband Dave.

Working in her office, she'd heard about SendOutCards as a tool for her insurance business. She wasn't interested, partly because of her negative impression of multilevel marketing. But while she was in the hospital, Kim received a follow-up call about SendOutCards. A few days later a heartfelt card showed up in the mail — along with an issue of *Success From Home* Magazine. Dave read it, Kim read it, and they signed up the next day.

"It totally opened up my eyes to a way to work from home without all the stress I was experiencing in my full-time job, which also took me away from my husband and two young daughters," she said.

Now an Executive, Kim said she wonders where she'd be today if Send-OutCards hadn't come along. "It provided us with much-needed income at a time when I was put on medical leave from my full-time job. It gave us a chance to focus on the positive things we could be grateful for in spite of being in a difficult situation, and it allowed us to have hope in a time that was very scary for us," she said.

"I AM" PHYSICALLY FIT AND HEALTHY

· MEGAN HAMLIN ·

After nine years of marriage Megan Hamlin was happy with her husband Ryan but wasn't feeling great about herself. During the newlywed years she gained 30 pounds, and after having babies she added a little more. "I had a total of 50-ish pounds of unhealthy extra," she said.

But when she made a decision to attend a Treat'em Right seminar in Las Vegas, everything changed; without expecting it, that trip became a turning point in her life. Faced with writing an "I am" statement and getting to the "why" that makes her cry, Megan jotted, "I am physically fit and healthy."

The following week was Thanksgiving 2010, and the self-imposed beginning of her journey. By early January she had lost 34 pounds and embarked on another goal to lose 10 additional pounds by her 10th anniversary in June 2011. And she did it.

Not only did she lose the weight, Megan was also able to run a half marathon with Ryan, who was working on his own "I am" fitness statement. "We are living the life we want because of this business," she said.

A WELL OF PREPARATION

· ROB MENDEZ ·

R ob Mendez got laid off in May. But this time was different than the first, three years ago.

That time, while working at his desk for a global financial-services firm, Rob got the dreaded tap on the shoulder and was told his job would end in two weeks. "I thought to myself, what happened to all that talk about converting me to an employee? What about my pregnant wife? What about my son? How am I going to provide for my family?"

With two days left at work, a co-worker spoke up for his performance during a conference call with the company vice president, and Rob's contract was extended.

After getting a gift like that, Rob wanted to do more than say thanks, so he resolved to buy a "thank you" card and get it in the mail. Four months passed before Rob actually bought the card at a grocery store. While he was waiting in line, he saw a magazine with Joel Osteen's name along the top edge. He bought it and the card, but once he was at home, he realized he had forgotten to buy a stamp.

Feeling frustrated, he started thumbing through the magazine — *Success From Home* — full of articles on a company called SendOutCards. He signed up as a distributor in September 2008 and scored his first wholesale customer almost immediately.

After a couple months, though, Rob's SendOutCards efforts waned, and when the financial markets took a tumble, he became a casualty of downsizing. "This was the third company I worked for in three years where I got laid off because of the company going bankrupt — just in time for Christmas. All my resources were tapped out by now — no more savings, no more lines of credit, no more 401(k)," he said.

And it was just the beginning. One 30-degree night in February, his family slept without heat because utilities had been turned off for non-payment. Rob was diagnosed with Type 2 diabetes. His house was on the brink of foreclosure, and the family sold their furniture just to make the car payment, knowing they could live in it if necessary.

Eighteen months later Rob found a job, but the salary wasn't enough. Recommitting himself to SendOutCards, he negotiated for the ability to work from home 70 percent of the time, which gave him flexibility to work on his SendOutCards business as well as pursue his passion — helping others better market themselves.

Within his first month of seriously diving into SendOutCards, he got his first distributor.

"When I first started SendOutCards, I took it seriously and got my first customer within a month. But then I slacked off. When I seriously got involved again, I got my first distributor. The learning point is that it really isn't difficult to get one customer and/or distributor a month if you take consistent action," Rob said.

And this spring, when his desk job disappeared, Rob was prepared.

"I dug my well before I was thirsty," Rob said. "I'm still building my SendOutCards business — one person and one card at a time. But now I don't have to be a victim anymore; I can send to give and know that I'll keep moving forward," he said.

THE POWER OF
THE WRITTEN WORD

· KAREN PUTZ ·

The first SendOutCards greeting card Karen Putz received was from a friend in Atlanta. The occasion was the death of Karen's father. When Karen opened the envelope, she found a photo of her hand holding her dad's, a shot she had taken just before he passed away. Karen had posted that photo on Facebook shortly before he died, and here it was, printed in a heartfelt card from a friend.

"Needless to say, I bawled. That card touched me the most because it really hit my heart," she said.

As a deaf woman, Karen knows the power of the written word, the power of putting feelings into text and images. Touched and intrigued by SendOutCards, Karen researched the company, and then joined. Today she's working on big ideas, like specialized videos in a card for those who use American Sign Language.

"I really enjoy creating cards and surprising folks here and there with a little appreciation and gratitude," she said. "With SendOutCards the possibilities are endless; the connections that result, priceless. Don't wait until it's too late."

IMPACTING LIVES WITH LAUGHTER

· EDIE HARDAGE ·

Edie Hardage had been out of touch with her aunt and uncle for several years when she received an e-mail with the news that her uncle had cancer and was not expected to live much longer.

Edie called her aunt, and told her she and her husband Gerald would be passing through in a few weeks; she asked her aunt if they could stop by for a visit.

That stop turned out to be a good night, with delicious Louisiana gumbo, lots of laughs, and plenty of photos. When Edie got home, she wanted to send a photo card, and Gerald wanted in on the action.

"He loves taking pictures and 'fixing' them in Photoshop — making long noses, big ears, pointed chins, that kind of thing," Edie said. It seemed a perfect match for Edie's aunt and uncle, who are "crazy people" who like to laugh, she said. Gerald fixed up a photo of Edie's aunt, and they included the photo in their card.

A few days later Edie's aunt called. She had received several cards in the mail that day, including Edie's, which was quickly given to Edie's uncle.

"She said that when he looked at the front of the card — that was my conservative picture — he grinned," Edie said. "Then he opened the card up and saw that ugly picture of my aunt that my husband had 'fixed up.' She said, 'Edith, he let out a big belly laugh. He thought that was the funniest thing.' Then she paused for a moment and with a cracked voice she said, 'Edith, it has been a long time since I have heard him laugh like that. I just want to say thank you for the card.'"

It was the last time Edie's aunt heard her husband laugh like that; he died just a few weeks later.

"I never intended for that card with that ugly, funny-looking picture to have such an impact on my uncle, my aunt, or me! But it did," Edie said. "My aunt keeps that card by her bed and remembers his big belly laugh. That would have never happened without SendOutCards. I would have thought about sending a card, maybe I would have even gone to the store and bought one. But I would never have taken the time to create a card that would make such an impact."

THE ESSENCE
OF SENDOUTCARDS

· TOMMY WYATT ·

Every day begins the same way for Tommy Wyatt: He sits down at his desk and sends someone a heartfelt greeting card. One day a couple months ago, he noticed an old friend on his Facebook account — someone he used to work with but hadn't spoken to in more than 20 years.

"I figured it would be nice to communicate with her and see how she was doing," Tommy said. "So I went onto her Facebook account and took a picture of her with her daughters and tried to put it onto the front of the card. However, the picture wasn't a high enough resolution to stretch across the entire front, so I tried to find a template that would fit the picture's size."

Tommy found just one template that would work with the size of the photo —a picture of a lighthouse and at the bottom, the words "I Am." So using that template, he put together a nice card and included a message, telling his friend he hoped she was doing well, that he appreciated her, and then sent the card, not thinking much of it again.

A couple of weeks later, Tommy received a nice message from her, sent via Facebook. Her note read, "I was just telling my mom last night, and

I've been meaning to write you but I keep forgetting — I loved the card! The funny thing is, my grandmother loved lighthouses. The cover picture is me and my girls in New Hampshire, on a trip to visit her. She passed away a few weeks ago while we were with her. Thankfully, we got to her in time to be with her and hold her hand as she passed. I've been thinking about her a lot lately and wondering if she's watching over us, hoping that she's happy and with her husband, my grandfather. I had just asked for a sign that she was okay, and in the mailbox, 'I Am.'"

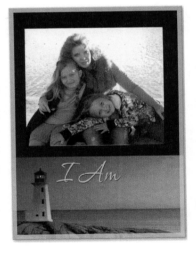

"That's the essence of SendOut-Cards," Tommy said.

ESTABLISHING WORK RELATIONSHIPS

• STEVE AND GAYLE ZIENTEK •

Steve and Gayle Zientek are Realtors with new marketing tools of choice: greeting cards and brownies.

Last summer the couple received a call from a woman, Mary, who was considering listing her home and was referred to them by a friend. Steve and Gayle met Mary, toured her home and property, and sent her a PicturePlus card loaded with photos of her home and gardens and a note that said, "Mary, you have a beautiful home. Let us know if we can be of further service." Brownies accompanied that card.

Mary called to say thanks but had decided it wasn't time to sell. However, she recommended that Steve and Gayle speak to her parents, who own a 65-acre farm in a nearby town. The Zienteks made the visit and sent the follow-up card, but the potential customers decided to wait for housing values to rebound.

Fast forward to June 2011. "My phone rings — it's Mary letting me know she'll be ready to list the house in about three weeks," Gayle said. "She also mentioned that Mom and Dad are not getting any younger and they will most likely be calling us in a couple months to come back over."

All it took was a thoughtful card and a tasty treat to begin that relationship with Mary and her folks. It's a formula that's worked for Steve and Gayle over and over again.

"I want to encourage all Realtors who may be reading this story to realize that a small token of appreciation can go a long way. Spending time creating a genuine heartfelt card can be instrumental in establishing a connection with someone you don't know very well. SendOutCards gives every Realtor in the world an opportunity to connect with their clients in a special way and build their businesses by simply sending one card at a time," Gayle said.

REIGNITING LOVE FOR LIFE

· NIKOLE THOMPSON ·

Nikole Thompson works as a caregiver for Cheryl, who has multiple sclerosis, a disease that has confined her to a bed. In August of 2009, one of Cheryl's former co-workers stopped by to visit her old friend. Nikole was there.

"I got to talk with her former co-worker, who was all fired up about this new company she was working with, called SendOutCards," Nikole said. The woman told Nikole a little about the service and then encouraged her to send a free card and watch the video. Nikole was busy at the time, so she put it off for a month or so. But within that month, Cheryl started receiving cards in the mail.

Little did Nikole know that Cheryl's friend had posted Cheryl's challenge with MS on the SendOutCards website, and distributors were reaching out to her patient with cards of love and encouragement.

"She would light up every time she received a new card," Nikole said. "I was impressed by the variety of cards she received, which prompted me to see what this company was all about. After I watched the video I was hooked, and my patient signed up as well."

Nikole loves SendOutCards, she said, but what it does for her patient is nothing short of a miracle.

"She was able to get her signature on file right before she lost use of her last limb," Nikole said. "It gives her a love for life again. She enjoys sending and receiving cards so much. In fact, this year for Christmas she got more cards than ever before."

For now, they are sending cards every chance they get.

"She has inspired me to be a better person through her kindness to others," Nikole said. "Her desire to keep in touch with people from her church, who she has not seen for 10 years but noticed their name on the prayer panel, is such a selfless act to witness. For those moments, and for SendOutCards, I am so grateful!"

WE'RE YOUR FAMILY; WE'RE HERE FOR YOU

· BRUCE FAIRCLOUGH ·

About the same time Bruce Fairclough started his SendOutCards business, his son married a lovely girl. Bruce was still getting to know his daughter-in-law six months later when her younger sister — the maid of honor at his son's wedding — was killed in an auto accident. She was just 21.

Bruce and his wife went to the funeral, where their daughter-in-law was to deliver the eulogy. "I really had no idea how she was going to get through it without falling apart. Yet she did — and did a beautiful job," Bruce said.

Driving home from the cemetery Bruce told his wife he had a prompting to send their daughter-in-law a card. This is part of what he wrote:

"I am writing to you as a daughter. My daughter.

"I have been getting used to that whole concept for some time now, but I didn't really know how much it was in my heart until I felt it last Tuesday in church watching you give your sister's eulogy.

"My heart suffered for you as any parent's heart would ache to see their child in pain. How many times, watching our children grow up and seeing them hurting, Mom and I would say we wished we could take the pain away and suffer it for them. My heart felt that watching you, knowing how much it hurt for you to deliver those words you felt for your baby sister.

"It appeared to me that (your sister) was the type of person that brought people together. I suspect that she will continue to do that in her passing. Let that be her legacy to our extended family, and more especially, to her big sister. We will always make sure our future grandchildren know who their 'auntie' was and know how important a person she was in the family.

"Finally, please know that we are your family. You can depend on us as parents, as friends, as a place to place your burdens, your sorrows, your joy, your laughter, your tears. We want you to know you are one of us now, and we are yours. We are here for you. Love, Pops."

But the really important part happened a couple weeks later at a Mother's Day dinner. It was the first time the family had been together since the funeral. "She and my son walked in, and as everyone was saying hello, she came right over to me, gave me a big hug and very quietly in my ear said, 'Thanks for the card, Pops.'

"It was the first time she had ever called me 'Pops' — a term of endearment with me in our family. Ever since then she's truly been one of the family — and more recently the mother of twins, our first grandbabies," Bruce said. "One thing that bothers me is when someone says that SendOutCards is not 'personal' because you don't actually handwrite in the card yourself. Here is the story I offer as proof that is not the case."

SENDING HOPE

· MELINDA RUSSELL ·

The winter of 2008 wasn't an easy one for Melinda Russell. A week after Thanksgiving she had foot surgery. The next week her sister unexpectedly passed away. And after Christmas her son Ben was sent to federal prison. Before the turmoil began, she'd joined SendOutCards, and at a friend's insistence, she started sending cards again. The first recipient was Ben.

Ben's cell mate was Vito, a 50-something man who had been in prison for years and would be there long after Ben was out. Vito mentioned how lucky Ben was to receive cards from home and from people who cared. So at Ben's request, Melinda sent Vito a "thinking of you" card with a quick hello and a few details about herself and her husband Mark.

A few days later she received a letter, five pages long and written front-and-back, from a return address at the prison. "In the letter Vito talked about how grateful he was to have someone he could write his feelings to, because in prison you have to be very careful who you trust and who you make yourself vulnerable to," Melinda said. "After I read Mark the letter he said, 'You have to write him back.'"

Since then Melinda has sent Vito many cards and gotten many letters back. Those letters overflow with thanks for becoming a part of his life — the only people, in fact, who care. In one letter Vito wrote, "I feel that my life has a purpose because I have something to look forward to rather than how I was feeling before you all came into my life. You have given my heart a reason to smile and face each day with that feeling in my heart, and that past emptiness is gone."

Things are looking up for Melinda too. Ben has been out of jail for a year, has a job he loves, and is getting married in October. And making Vito's life a little brighter has made hers brighter too. "If you think that sending one card does not change someone's life, this is my proof that it does," Melinda said. "There are happy endings."

BRINGING
BROTHERS TOGETHER

· MICHAEL QUARANTI AND ANTHONY BAMBINO ·

Forty-two years ago Anthony Bambino was born into a difficult and desperate situation, the son of two young and poor parents in the Bronx who split up before he turned one. Raised by his father, Anthony saw his mother, a factory worker who fought poverty and suffered drug addiction, a few times a year. As he got older, he realized his mother was high during most his visits.

When Anthony turned 12, his mom gave birth to her second son, a boy she named Michael Quaranti. "I remember it like it was yesterday, going to her apartment with my grandmother the week my brother was born," Anthony said. "When we walked in, my grandmother was quite upset because my mother was obviously high and should not have been alone with a newborn baby. But what I remember most was holding this newborn, cute little baby who was my brother. I was 12 years old, and was hoping that this new baby might give my mother a reason to get clean."

Things didn't turn out as Anthony had hoped. The next year his mother overdosed on heroin in a rundown hotel. Michael, then a toddler, moved with his father to his aunt's house in the Bronx, while Anthony was living in Connecticut. For a decade the two hardly saw each other.

At age 14, Michael was growing up in the Little Italy section of the Bronx, where he frequented social clubs with bars, pool tables, and card rooms. Before long he started gambling, and once he was introduced to sports betting, things got serious. "I developed a bad gambling addiction, and I didn't know how to control it," he said.

Meanwhile Anthony was trying to reach out to Michael, but the age gap and time spent apart had taken its toll. When all was said and done, the brothers saw each other less and less. Michael, then 17, picked up a job as a doorman and tried Gamblers Anonymous, but the old addiction kept creeping back into this life. For 12 years he fought it, but he knew he needed something big — something positive — to get him on the right track once and for all.

So it was a fortunate day November 26, 2010, when Anthony called Michael and invited him over. Once there Anthony introduced Send-OutCards, the business that had been his own saving grace when his construction business, along with the economy, took a nosedive, losing 85 percent of business almost overnight. Michael was a quick study.

"After going over the opportunity with (Anthony) for a few hours, I instantly saw the vision of where this company was going. I signed up on the spot," Michael said.

Even Anthony was amazed at how the company brought them together. "We just found the bridge that was missing in our lives for the past 29 years! I would have never imagined when I was introduced to SendOut-Cards that this is not only a vehicle for financial freedom, but this was the vehicle for my brother and I to have the relationship we were robbed of our entire lives because our mom had passed away," he said.

After Michael joined, the brothers dove in together, and within four and a half months, both were Senior Managers. "Since the day my brother joined, our lives have changed 180 degrees," Anthony said. "We speak to each other approximately three times a day, and it is all about SendOutCards and strategizing and working on building our teams and downlines and trying to motivate our downlines to succeed. We have become very close friends above and beyond what most brothers experience."

A VIDEO ANTIDOTE FOR LONG DISTANCE

· TRACEY DEAN ·

Growing up is hard, and it's further complicated when a loved one leaves the nest for faraway skies — and misses major family events as a result.

Tracey Dean saw this firsthand when a family friend named Steve came to say goodbye before shipping out on his summer tour with the Maritime Academy. "He was telling me that his sister Alex was really upset because he wouldn't be able to be there when she graduated high school," Tracey said. "Steve really felt bad about this. I thought for a moment and said, 'Well, you can be there, in a way.'"

The two set out to craft a video card. Steve and Tracey's two sons made a video for Alex, Steve selected and personalized a graduation card, and SendOutCards did the rest. The card arrived the day before Alex's graduation.

"(Alex's) mom called me yesterday and thanked me for helping Steve make the wonderful card," Tracey said. "She said that Alex cried when she watched the video and has shown it to all her friends. She also said that they pull out the card and watch the video when they're missing Steve. I would say that was a complete success!"

WORDS OF STRENGTH IN DIFFICULT TIMES

• VICKI MCCUTCHAN •

A lifelong card sender, Vicki McCutchan knew the power of a card. But last year, even Vici was surprised by the difference a card can make.

On April 16, 2010, Vicki's 37-year-old stepson Jon was walking near his home in Maryland when he was struck and killed by an impaired motorist.

Just 18 days prior, Jon had been sent on a work trip to Dallas, close enough to Vicki's home in Bastrop, Texas, that she and her husband Tom could hook up the trailer and head north for a quick visit.

"We were going to take him out to dinner, but he wanted to come hang at camp with us and have a home-cooked meal," Vicki said. "What a great visit we had, telling him how proud we were of him and how much we loved him. And the sunset that evening was glorious, and I got the most beautiful photo of Jon and Tom."

When they got the devastating call that their Jon was gone, they cried until their bodies ached, and Vicki said they wondered if they would ever smile or laugh again.

Then the cards started arriving, greeting cards with words of love and support from friends and family. "As each one arrived we would sit together, and I would read them out loud and then place them somewhere in the living room," Vicki said.

As the days passed, more cards arrived, until more than 40 cards were placed around the living room.

"We felt the strength of those shared words of love lifting us up and helping us to get on with our life," she said.

Finally the day came when Vicki and Tom were strong enough to read them all out loud again, one by one, and then place them in a box and put them away. "We have more conviction than ever of the power of the words shared in cards, expressed from the heart, and we are grateful," she said.

REBUILDING OLD RELATIONSHIPS

· JENNIFER ELKIN ·

SendOutCards has been the means for getting Jennifer Elkin back where she was as a child.

Jennifer grew up on an idyllic 50-acre family farm called The Homestead. Both sets of grandparents worked the land, and once her parents married, they built a home on the apple orchard property. Jennifer grew up surrounded by aunts, uncles, cousins, and grandparents.

"We played together, went to school together, and lived life together," Jennifer said. "Our grandparents had a home on the corner, and I remember vividly how we would celebrate every holiday there, and we would walk to grandma and grandpa's for breakfast on the weekend. I remember going there on Thanksgiving morning, so that we could watch the Macy's Day parade in color."

But that lifestyle was interrupted when Jennifer fell ill as a child and the family relocated to Fort Lauderdale, Florida. "Although the move was exciting, it was also devastating because we were going to miss everyone," Jennifer said.

As years passed, Jennifer tried to keep in touch with relatives, but her wedding 16 years ago was the last time the family was together.

When Jennifer found SendOutCards, she knew she had found a way to keep in touch with loved ones. Better yet, she had found the vehicle that would take her to visit them.

Since starting her SendOutCards business, Jennifer has traveled the country visiting relatives and building relationships that started in her youth. She's also been able to help loved ones financially, thanks to her income.

And she has more goals. The next one is to "gather our big Italian family again and have a big reunion," she said. In fact, she's got an "I am" statement to help get her there.

"We love SendOutCards and the freedom to dream and build our relationships again! We are forever grateful for SendOutCards helping us rekindle many relationships and putting a bigger purpose behind it all," Jennifer said.

LIVING A LIFE
OF FREEDOM

· BEN FITTS ·

B en Fitts has a SendOutCards story that begins like most: He was married, had a full-time job, and had another part-time home business. "I never intended to do SendOutCards as an actual business," Ben said. "I saw it as a way to grow my other business." Originally, it was a quick, easy, and cost-effective way to get more referrals and repeat sales.

"Then a funny thing happened," Ben said. "A young lady named Diane Walker received a birthday card from me. We had been working together in my other business, become trainers, and exchanged birthdays and addresses with one another. I started sending birthday cards to her to show my appreciation for all she did. At the time, the only gifts Send-OutCards had were $25 gift cards that included 20 points and enough postage to send 10 cards. That's what I sent Diane and everyone else I was sending birthday cards to. When Diane received my card she called and asked, 'What are you trying to recruit me into?' I don't remember my exact answer but it was something along the line of, "Nothing, don't worry about it. I just wanted to send you a birthday card."

Six weeks later Ben got another call from Diane. She said it was eating away at her that Ben had spent $25 on a gift for her, so she used it to see what SendOutCards was all about.

"She told me that as soon as she logged onto SendOutCards, she immediately fell in love with it. She noticed there was an opportunity associated with it, and was naturally curious," Ben said.

Diane's curiosity had piqued Ben's as well and he decided to start working his own SendOutCards business in earnest. It turned out to be a great move, as his old business shut down shortly thereafter.

"SendOutCards has impacted my life in so many positive ways," Ben said. "It has helped me grow personally from attending the seminars and conventions. I've met some of the best people in the world, read awesome books from the SendOutCards online selection, and I've had the opportunity to share our cards with all types of people. In my seven years with SendOutCards, many things have changed in my life, but SendOutCards has been there the whole time. I don't know where I would be today if not for SendOutCards.

"I truly live a life of freedom, I don't have to set an alarm clock and I don't hate going to work. I have the freedom to choose where and when I work. How many other people have that flexibility? This is why, to me, SendOutCards truly means freedom."

LIFE IS A JOURNEY

• BRAD HORTON •

A couple of years ago, Brad Horton's mother-in-law was admitted to an assisted living center in the small Australian town where she lived. Prior to this she had lived on her brother's farm in Stroud, New South Wales, for 40 years. It was a beautiful place with rolling green hills, creeks, and fresh air. His wife was able to visit her mother every year for a couple of weeks, but in between, she was indeed half a world away.

As time passed, Brad felt it would be a great idea to send his mother-in-law cards regularly. "A son-in-law sending his mother-in-law cards — now there's a twist!" Brad said. So he began sending PicturePlus cards of grandchildren, great-grandchildren, and of course, her daughters.

On Father's Day, the family received news that she was not doing well and her time could be very near. "My wife and I made the decision to make an impromptu airline reservation to Australia. Five hours before we landed in Sydney she passed away," Brad said.

A couple of days after the funeral, the couple went to her room at the center to move some furniture and personal belongings. "She was not one to hold onto many things — clutter, she called it," Brad said. "But there in her room were all the cards I had sent her over the years. At that moment I realized one of the most important missions of SendOut-Cards, even though I was halfway around the world: A life was touched, a smile was made. We did not miss her by five hours; we were with her in those cards. Life is a journey and ours is better when it changes a life, one card at a time."

HOW SHE GOT HER WINGS

• CHRISTINE REID •

Christine Reid was new in SendOutCards, and faithfully doing what she learned the leaders in the company did. Her upline, Jeff Packard, invited her to listen in on a weekly Senior Manager call he was having, even though she had not yet achieved that goal. "Although I was intimidated by those weekly calls and the energetic, successful people I met there, it also encouraged me to work even harder to build my business," Christine said.

In December 2007, while she was looking through the SendOutCards website, she found herself diverted to the Eagles Challenge section. "I knew that the top 100 would win cruises so I looked to see who those lucky people were. As I read down the list I saw the distributors that I would call the 'Hall of Fame' of SendOutCards' sales leaders. I was shocked when I arrived at #112 and saw my own name on this list. I couldn't believe my eyes! To make sure I was reading it correctly, I backed out of the page and came back several times."

Christine became re-energized when she realized how close she was to winning that cruise. As further motivation to push hard to get into the top 100, Christine bought plane tickets to the cruise site in Florida for herself and her husband.

"I hate wasting money, but I felt this would push me into doing everything possible to win that spot," Christine said. "On the next team call with Jeff we talked about our goals, which prompted me to tell the people on the call that I had already purchased my airline tickets for Florida, even though I was not in the top 100." Christine continued to work hard, and saw herself winning the cruise.

On the last day of this contest, she was still a few spots out of the top 100 with only hours remaining in the challenge. As the hours ticked by, a new member joined her team, bumping her into the top 100.

"My heart skipped a beat a few days later when I got an email from SendOutCards corporate telling me that I had won the trip!" Christine said. "That was the day I got my wings and realized I could achieve my goals."

IT STARTED
WITH A MOVIE

· DENNIS WARD ·

Dennis Ward's initial motivation for building a SendOutCards business was simply to make enough money to spoil his grandchildren a bit. "Three years ago, when I first started with SendOutCards, I got my first commission check. I thought, 'This is a great business!' Even if all I could ever make was enough money to take my grandkids to the movies each month and spoil them with popcorn and candy, this would be an awesome business." So he cashed his commission check, and used it to take four of his grandchildren to the movies.

A few months went by, and he found that not only could he take the grandkids to the movies, he could also make a car payment with his check from SendOutCards. A few months later, he discovered he could take the grandkids to the movies, make his car payment, and also pay his mortgage.

"A couple of months later, I got a text from Burke Christensen, congratulating me on a $600 day. Naturally I asked, 'What happened?' He told me they brought four people in that day. My first thought was to feel a little guilty because I wasn't there to 'own' that money. However, my second thought reassured me: That's how it's supposed to be. I'm supposed to bring people in, they bring people in, and I get paid. That's my story with SendOutCards, and that's what works for me."

STAYING IN TOUCH WITH SENDOUTCARDS

• JEANETTE MCVOY •

Jeanette McVoy had a busy career as a pediatric nurse for 39 years before becoming the owner of a traditional small business. About that same time, her husband Joe began using SendOutCards to stay in touch with his customers. "I decided to give SendOutCards a try," Jeanette said. "I loved the SendOutCards opportunity so much I decided to start building my own business."

A short while after beginning her SendOutCards business, she used greeting cards to help invite family —many of whom had been out of touch for a long time — to a reunion. Joe and Jeanette have four grown children, five grandchildren, and live in Colorado, but were reaching out to some 60 relatives in Kansas. "If past years were any indication I had no idea how many people would actually show up," Jeanette said. "I was shocked when over 100 people were there, including all five of my living aunts and three uncles, all in their 90s. Most of them had not seen each other for over 30 years. SendOutCards even brought my sister and me back together."

SendOutCards has also changed her business life for the better. In just a few short years, she is earning double what she made as a full-time RN — and she is still working just part-time. "It's definitely one of the best decisions I've ever made!" Jeanette said.

A SIMPLE ACT OF APPRECIATION

· LINDA LEQUESNE ·

Linda LeQuesne shares the power of a heartfelt card that crossed a language barrier and helped her make a new friend. "I had only been using SendOutCards for about a month when I went to get my hair cut at a walk-in salon where no appointment is needed," she said. "I always had the same hairdresser, but we didn't talk much during my haircutting sessions due to a language barrier."

After a particular appointment, Linda was admiring her new haircut in the mirror at home, and felt a prompting to send her hairdresser, Molly, a card. She chose a nice "thank you" card from the card catalog and wrote, "Molly, Thank you for giving me consistently great haircuts. I really appreciate you! Sincerely, Linda." She put her picture on the left side of the card so Molly would know who had sent the card.

About a month later, in need of another haircut, Linda set off for the same salon. "When I walked into the salon Molly was at her desk with her head down. When she saw me at the door her eyes lit up; she ran around the counter and gave me the biggest hug," Linda said.

With tears in her eyes, Molly told her, in halting English, "Thank you! Nobody ever send me card like that. Mean so much to me!" And there was Linda's card, taped in the center of Molly's mirror.

"I had no idea what an impact one little card could have on someone," Linda said. "I vowed then and there to act on every prompting, and that I will let the people in my life know how much I appreciate them."

A BIRTHDAY TO REMEMBER

• HEATHER ROUILLARD •

Everyone has a golden birthday once in a lifetime —it's the day you turn your age on the date of your birthday. For Heather Rouillard, that date was April 29.

"I found out that I was going to share my 29th birthday — my golden birthday — with my beautiful sister's graduation ceremony," Heather said. Her sister's husband had been deployed to Iraq for a good part of the time her sister had been in school, leaving her sister to raise two young boys alone while finishing school. Needless to say, her sister's graduation was deserving of a full day of recognition from the entire family! So Heather and her family flew from Minnesota to New Mexico to celebrate her sister's special day.

"I was very excited for her ceremony and party, but still a bit deflated that I had to share my golden birthday with someone else," Heather said.

Heather's best friend Molly had a hunch that Heather may feel her special day getting lost in the other celebration. So Molly got the address in New Mexico where the family would gather for the graduation ceremony and hatched a plan to make Heather's day special too.

"We were all at my sister's house when my nephew came running down the street yelling, 'Auntie, auntie, you got some letters, a LOT of them,'" Heather remembered. As her nephew ran up to her, his hands were completely full of mail — all SendOutCards postcards sent by Molly. Some were pictures from college with a personal memory, others were photos of various people with personal messages —all were sweet, hilarious, or just completely random.

"She ended up sending me 29 postcards for my 29th birthday on April 29th," Heather said. "I have never received such a sweet gesture, and at that moment they were exactly what I needed. She made me feel like I was the most important person in the world."

"I AM" A THIRD WORLD SCHOOL BUILDER

· DAVID FREY ·

"I am a third world school builder." That was David Frey's "I am" statement before he even knew what an "I am" statement was. His idea formed roots in 1989 while David was on a mission for his church in Bolivia, the second-poorest country in the Americas.

"My heart broke for many of the children who lived out in the rural areas of the country because they were so poor that they could not afford to go to school. And even when schools were offered, many children could not attend because it was too far to walk and they couldn't afford bicycles," he said.

David promised himself he would someday build a school for impoverished children. He even drew a picture of what that school would look like. When he returned to the States, he framed the picture and hung it in his kitchen as a reminder. But for a long time, building a school remained a lofty dream.

"As the years passed, I would look at that drawing and tell myself, 'Maybe next year.' I had that drawing hanging up in my kitchen for nearly 20 years," David said. "Each year I told myself, 'Next year.'"

At the 2007 SendOutCards convention, David attended a "back to the future" party where guests were asked to dress in something representing where they wanted to be in five years.

"I knew where I wanted to be in five years, and it had nothing to do with exotic locations, fancy cars, income levels, status, ranking, or any of those things," David said. "I knew that in five years I wanted to be a third world school builder. So I had a special shirt created that said, 'I AM a Third World School Builder.'"

He wore the shirt several times after that dinner was over, and it wasn't long until he had a powerful impression to stop procrastinating and to put his plan in action. Now he just needed to know how.

Within a week he got that answer when a friend called and told him about a charity called World Teacher Aid. David was asked to be a board member, and his dream began turning into reality.

WTA was already funding feeding programs and teachers' salaries in Kenya and Uganda, and David immediately started planning a school. After cutting through lots of red tape, WTA opened its school in March — one year prior to David's five-year "back to the future" goal — in a small village outside Nakuru, Kenya.

The school is named Shalom Primary School, after the Hebrew word for "peace," and is situated in a Kenyan refugee encampment.

"In 2008 Kenya's presidential elections incited riots and eventually mass murders," David said. "The fighting got so bad that the government decided to move hundreds of thousands of people to barren land in other parts of the country where there were no buildings, no running water, no electricity, nothing. Our school was the very first school created to serve these people."

The eight-classroom school can accept as many as 50 students per classroom. More than 3,000 villagers showed up to celebrate the inauguration of the school, as did Kenya's secretary of education, secretary of internal programs, the provincial governor, and other local politicians and dignitaries.

This is only the beginning for David; his goal is to build one school a year through WTA.

"I could never have built this school without SendOutCards," he said. "The money that was used to build part of this school came from the residual income that SendOutCards sends to me each and every week. I call it the school that SendOutCards built. So today, along with being a husband, a dad and a proud SendOutCards distributor, I am officially a third world school builder. My dream came true through the power of the 'I am.'"

STORY
OF MY LIFE

· LOU-ANNE HUNT ·

Lou-Anne Hunt met Wayne Hunt on June 4, 2005, through a friend who owned a dating service. "It was on that first date that I knew I would be with Wayne forever," she remembers. And so began a Cinderella fairytale that little girls dream of, each page filled with a growing friendship, marriage, and a blossoming love story.

A few short months later, Wayne was diagnosed with A.L.S. (Amyotrophic Lateral Sclerosis — Lou Gehrig's disease), a form of motor neuron disease that affects every muscle in the body. Those who have this disease retain their memory, senses, and awareness, while their body shuts down. There is no cure for A.L.S. and it is still inconclusive what causes this disease or how it progresses.

"When you find out that your loved one has a disease, you become an expert in that disease," Lou-Anne said. "I found myself completely immersed, focused on any promise of a cure and, I also became an expert caregiver."

In early diagnoses, Wayne seem to slowly show signs and symptoms. "I was so busy making sure that his every wish and dream was granted I didn't realize how fast time flies," Lou-Anne said. "Wayne's final wish was to die at home. In November 2007 he took a deep breath and let out a final sigh." A tough battle had been won – by A.L.S. Lou-Anne's world spiraled downward into darkness and depression.

Two years later, after watching the movie *The Secret,* Lou-Anne had a strong feeling her life was about to change. Finally, she was on the road to recovery. This change would turn out to be a new personal development journey for her, while she journaled and discovered her true self once again. She was no longer the grieving widow, caregiver, or controller. At about this time, Lou-Anne heard of SendOutCards and soon became a Distributor.

"I attended my first SendOutCards Convention in September 2010. At the opening ceremonies, a video of a soaring eagle began to play and the room filled with energy," she said. "When the lights came up after the video, a live eagle, Challenger, made one amazing swoop, and flew just inches over the heads of the audience. His wingspan was breathtaking. It was a truly unforgettable display of beauty and grace and a moment that will inspire me for many years to come."

Shortly after that convention, Lou-Anne attended the Detroit Treat'em Right. At the point where Kody asks the audience to write a heartfelt greeting card, Lou-Anne knew immediately which card she would write. It was nearly the third anniversary of Wayne's death, and the words flowed onto her card. Kody called for volunteers to read their cards to the audience; Lou-Anne was selected and read her card for the crowd. Then Kody called her to the stage.

"As I stood before my peers, I lived a dream that day — standing on the stage with Kody Bateman telling 'The Story of My Life.' As Kody asked the audience to give Wayne an unforgettable standing ovation I found myself overcome with gratitude and appreciation," Lou-Anne said.

When she got home she sat down at her computer and created the "Story of my Life" greeting card, smiling as she uploaded pictures of Hawaii and their wedding.

"I sent a copy to Kody and thanked him for the standing ovation, all the time wondering if Kody would even receive my card because he receives so many," she said. "Imagine my surprise when one day after work I received a greeting card from Kody, thanking me for sharing my story!"

MY SENDOUTCARDS STORY